The Secret of How Dangoma Became a Billionaire

Anthony Osae-Brown

Illustrated by Kingsley Nkor

AuthorHouse™
1663 Liberty Drive
Bloomington, IN 47403
www.authorhouse.com
Phone: 1 (800) 839-8640

Illustrated by Kingsley Nkor.

Published by AuthorHouse 02/05/2016

ISBN: 978-1-5049-7783-8 (sc)
ISBN: 978-1-5049-7784-5 (e)

Library of Congress Control Number: 2016901947

Print information available on the last page.

This is a work of fiction. All of the characters, names, incidents, organizations, and dialogue in
this novel are either the products of the author's imagination or are used fictiously.

For KK and Maya

Table of Contents

Chapter 1

Dangoma, the Daydreamer

Dangoma lived life as a daydreamer. In his greatest daydreams, he wondered what it would take to be as wealthy as his uncle, who was known everywhere as a very rich man with many successful businesses.

His uncle's name was Shangisha. He was Dangoma's maternal uncle. He was known far and wide for his business wisdom. He owned many businesses, and many people worked for him. Dangoma's mother often took him to visit Uncle Shangisha in his big house located on the outskirts of the city. The house had many rooms, and Dangoma sometimes got lost just trying to find his way from one room to another.

Often, Uncle Shangisha would ask Dangoma to sit in one of his very comfortable chairs, which always swallowed him up because the cushions were so soft and big, and then he would tell Dangoma exciting stories about running a business. Dangoma got used to Uncle Shangisha talking about his businesses, and he started feeling like he could run a business too – even though he was just ten years old. In short, after hearing his uncle's words, he could not wait to start a business of his own. As he went to bed one night, he made the decision to visit his uncle the next morning to make a request. He wanted to run his own business as soon as possible and felt confident he could do it.

Chapter 2

Dangoma Asks to Start a Business

The next morning, Dangoma visited Uncle Shangisha in his big house to make his request to start a business. Uncle Shangisha was seated in one of his comfortable chairs and reading the morning newspaper, but as soon as he saw Dangoma, he dropped the paper and stood up.

"Dangoma, how are you today?" Uncle Shangisha asked as he hugged the boy.

"I am fine," Dangoma answered.

"How is your mummy?"

"She is fine. She has gone to her shop."

The man and the boy looked at each other. Uncle Shangisha could see that Dangoma had something on his mind. "You are here early today. Do you have something to tell me?" Uncle Shangisha asked when he noticed that Dangoma seemed eager to speak.

"Yes, Uncle," Dangoma answered.

Dangoma had thought all night about how he was going to make his request, but now that he was with his uncle, he was not sure whether he should say anything.

"What is it that you want to say?" asked Uncle Shangisha.

"I want to start a business," Dangoma said hesitantly.

"That is interesting."

"Uncle, you have told me so much about how to run a business that I am confident I can successfully run one. I also want to have a business like you do," Dangoma said.

"Dangoma, I am happy to hear this. You sound very confident. But won't running a business divert your attention from your schoolwork?" Uncle Shangisha asked.

"No, I can fit it in after the school day is over."

"Have you told your mummy about it?"

"Yes. She says it is okay if you say it is okay," answered Dangoma.

"Dangoma, it is true that you do not have to wait until you are as old as I am before you start a business. You can start right now if you assure me that you will not be distracted from your schoolwork."

Now excited, Dangoma said, "Yes, Uncle, I assure you I will not be distracted from my schoolwork."

"Okay. But since this is going to be your first attempt at running a business, it is important to start small. Take five hundred naira (N500/$2.50) and do with it whatever comes to mind. In a week's time, let me know how much profit you have made."

"Thank you, Uncle. I promise that I will not disappoint you. I am going to make a lot of money from this," Dangoma said before taking the money from his uncle excitedly and running home.

When Dangoma got home, he told his mum about his conversation with Uncle Shangisha and the five hundred naira ($2.50) he had been given to start his first business.

"Mummy, I am going to make money. I am going to double this money, and I am going to make Uncle Shangisha proud," Dangoma said.

His mummy looked at him with a smile on her face. "I know you are going to make money, but what business are you going to create with the money?" she asked.

"I do not know yet, Mummy," Dangoma answered, looking puzzled.

"And how are you going to make money if you are not even sure about what business to do with the money?"

Dangoma became quite puzzled and asked, "Can you give me a suggestion?"

"If you are going to create a business, you have to think of a product that people are willing to pay for or are already paying for. The more people are willing to pay for a product, the more money you can make. Therefore, if you want to make money, think of a product that many people are going to buy from you happily," Dangoma's mummy advised.

She then continued: "Also, think of something that you will enjoy selling. If what you are going to sell is not something you like, you will not enjoy selling it. Therefore, sell what you would enjoy buying. That way, you will sell happily, and it will be easier for you to convince your customers to buy from you."

"Okay, Mummy," Dangoma said. His confidence was punctured a bit now that he realized he had no idea what business he was going to create with the money. And with that thought, he walked to his room quietly with his head down.

Chapter 4

Dangoma in Search of a Business Idea

Dangoma could not sleep that night. His eyes remained opened as he turned from one side to the other in his bed, trying to figure out what business was worthy of his uncle's five hundred naira ($2.50).

He could feel his heart pumping faster than usual as the fear of failing his uncle's challenge gripped him. All he could imagine was the disappointment that would show on his uncle's face if he were to tell him that he lost all the money he had been given.

Dangoma thought of all the things that could go wrong. He wondered whether he had not been in too much of a hurry to ask his uncle to give him money for a business. Perhaps I should have waited until I was twelve years old, he thought. The more he thought about the fact that he had no business idea yet, the more he became afraid.

Still gripped by his fear, Dangoma slipped quietly into a dream in which he set up a shop to sell some items he could not identify immediately. In the dream, many people passed his shop, but none of them stopped to buy anything.

He woke up feeling cold despite the fact that he was sweating. But he was not concerned about the sweating or coldness; he was more concerned that he still had no idea what type of business he was going to conduct with his uncle's five hundred naira ($2.50).

Chapter 5

Mummy Helps out with a Tip

"Good morning," Dangoma said to his mummy, who was busy serving breakfast.

"Good morning, Dangoma. I hope you slept well."

"Yes, Mummy."

"Do you now have that great business idea?"

"No, Mummy."

"Do not worry; it will come. Go and take your bath so that you can eat."

"Mummy, I do not want to take my bath. I just want a business idea," Dangoma replied as he sat down at the dining table.

"Dangoma, go take your bath. Sometimes great ideas come while cold water is running down your spine. The effect of the cold water can stimulate your thinking."

"Okay, I will go take my bath," Dangoma answered dutifully.

He felt desperate to come up with a business idea. After listening to his uncle talk about running a business every day, he did not realize it would be so difficult to decide what business to create.

"Dangoma, have you finished taking your bath?" his mummy asked later.

"No, but I am about to, Mummy."

To his surprise, it happened exactly as his mummy had said: as cool water ran down from his head to his spine, a business idea sprang into his head.

Dangoma's business idea was simple: he was going to buy packs of sweets and sell them in single units to his classmates in school. He knew all his classmates loved sweets, and during break time, they usually walked to the only kiosk in the school where sweets were sold.

With the idea burning in his head, he ran out of the bathroom to tell his mum.

"Mummy, Mummy, I have a great business idea now!" he exclaimed.

"What is it?"

"I am going to sell sweets. All my friends in school love sweets. I am going to sell sweets to them."

"That is great, but before you go off running to buy sweets, ask first why your friends would want to buy sweets from you instead of buying them from the usual place."

"They have to buy from me because they are my friends."

"No, Dangoma, business does not work that way. If the sweets you are going to sell them are more expensive than the sweets your friends buy now, they will soon stop buying sweets from you. Therefore, if you want your friends to buy sweets from you and continue buying from you, you must sell sweets that are cheaper than those they buy now or, better still, sweets that are cheaper and tastier than those they buy now" Dangoma's mummy said.

"But where will I get sweets that are cheaper than those my friends buy now?" asked Dangoma.

"You have to go into the open market and find out. I will send you to Alhaji Kaswa. He will be able to advise you on which sweets to sell," said Dangoma's mummy.

"Thank you, Mummy," said Dangoma

"Now eat. After you finish eating, you can go see Alhaji Kaswa."

"Okay, Mummy," answered Dangoma.

As Dangoma ate his breakfast, his mummy explained to him why he had to go the market to see Alhaji Kaswa.

"Dangoma, you already know the sweets your friends like and how many they buy. If you want to succeed in this business, you must do a feasibility study. Go into the main market and find out which other sweets are available. Find out whether they are tastier and cheaper than the ones your friends eat now. Find out how much it costs to buy the sweets, and then work out how much you can sell them for to your friends."

"When you get to the market, ask for Alhaji Kaswa. He is the biggest sweet merchant in the market. He will tell you all you need to know about sweets."

"Thank you, Mummy. I will go now," said Dangoma as he ran off towards the market.

Everyone knew Alhaji Kaswa, so it was not difficult for Dangoma to find his shop. As Dangoma walked into Alhaji Kaswa's shop, he was greeted by the sweet aroma of the different types of sweets he sold. The sweets were packed in different cartons from the floor all the way to the ceiling of the shop.

Alhaji Kaswa was busy rearranging the sweet cartons. Dangoma quickly introduced himself and the man said, "Is that you, Dangoma? What can I do for you?"

"I am here to buy some sweets to sell in school. My uncle gave me five hundred naira ($2.50), and he wants me to trade with it. He wants to see how much more money I can make on the five hundred naira ($2.50)."

"That is very good," Alhaji Kaswa said. "Which type of sweets do you want to buy?"

"My friends in school like Milky Nuts. I am sure that, if I buy them, I will be able to sell them easily."

"Milky Nuts! Yes, they taste great, but they are expensive. It costs two hundred and fifty naira ($1.25) per pack."

"Each pack has fifty sweets. If you buy a pack, the cost of each sweet will be five naira (2.5 cents)."

"But the stores in school sell them for ten naira (5 cents) each," Dangoma said.

Insert image 8

"Ten naira (5 cents) is the retail price. The wholesale price is five naira (2.5 cents). Thus, the retailer in your school adds five naira (2.5 cents) to each sweet," Alhaji Kaswa explained.

"But why is he adding so much money?"

"Since you want to go into business, you need to understand this. The price at which you buy the sweet is not the total cost of the sweet – it is just part of it. You have to take into consideration the cost of transportation. And as a trader, you have to look at how much you pay for rent and electricity to power the store. You have to take all these costs into consideration before you decide on the final price of the item you are selling. The actual cost of the sweet is equal to the cost of buying it, plus the cost of transportation, plus the cost of rent, plus the cost of electricity in your shop, plus the cost of any other expenses you encounter. After that, you add how much profit you want to make on the sweet to get the final price, which is the same as how much you decide to sell the sweet for.

"This sounds really complicated," Dangoma said.

"No, it is not. Anyone who wants to be a good business person must understand the concept of pricing very well; otherwise, the business will fail. Business is really about the right pricing of whatever you are selling. Every business must make enough money to cover the cost of staying in business and a little more as profit," Alhaji Kaswa explained

"I never thought of it that way. All I wanted to do was sell sweets, but now you are making business sound like a lot of mathematics," Dangoma said.

"Yes, business is a lot of mathematics. But the mathematics in business is called accounting. Accounting is a very interesting subject because it is about keeping a financial record of every item you put into your business. If you do not do that, your business will soon collapse. Every business owner must be able to give a proper account of his or her business every day. All money spent and earned must be recorded and accounted for in a business," Alhaji Kaswa said.

Chapter 8

Dangoma Decides Which Sweets to Buy

"Now let us go back to why you are here, Dangoma," Alhaji Kaswa said. "How much did you bring to buy the sweets?"

"I am here with five hundred naira ($2.50)," Dangoma answered.

"That means you can only buy two packs of sweets. How many sweets will that be?"

"That will be one hundred sweets because each pack has fifty sweets," Dangoma answered.

"That is good. So if you are going to sell each sweet for ten naira (5 cents), what will be the total sales?"

"That will be one thousand naira ($5)," Dangoma answered with a smile.

"Yes, you are right. That means you will have doubled the five hundred ($2.50) your uncle gave to you."

"Yes," Dangoma said, beaming. "And my uncle says if I double it, he will give me more money to trade with."

"Wait a little bit, Dangoma. Do not get excited yet. You have not sold the sweets yet. I want to ask you a question. Why would your friends buy sweets from you if you are selling them at the same price as the store in your school?"

"They are my friends, so they should buy from me," Dangoma answered.

"That is a good reason, but no business will exist for long depending on the unearned goodwill of friends. Friends are not necessarily customers. And customers are not necessarily your friends. If you want your friends to become customers, you must offer them something that no other shop can offer them. Or else, soon, they will go behind you to buy from the shop that offers them more value," Alhaji Kaswa explained.

"Okay, so what can I do to turn my friends into long-term customers?"

"Let us look at it this way: I am suggesting you sell your sweets at a lower price than the store in your school. Remember what I told you earlier? The things you have to consider before you decide on the final price of any item you want to sell?"

"Yes," Dangoma answered.

"In your case, many of those things do not apply. You are not going to sell your sweets from a shop, so you are not going to pay rent or electricity. Also, because your house is close to my shop, you do not have get transportation down here. This means that your cost is actually lower than the store in your school. Consequently, you can afford to sell your sweets at a lower price. Do you understand?"

"Yes, but that means I will not make as much money as the store in my school," Dangoma answered, shaking his head.

"You will actually make more money!" Alhaji Kaswa replied.

"How do I make more money when I am selling at a lower price?" Dangoma asked.

"That is the trick of volume. Selling at a lower price means that you can sell your sweets faster than the store in your school. For example, it may take you two weeks to sell your sweets if you are selling them at ten naira (5 cents) each. But it may take you a week to sell them if you sell at the lower price of eight naira (4 cents) per sweet. Do the mathematics: in two weeks, you will make one thousand naira ($5) in revenues at ten naira (5 cents) per sweet. At eight naira (4 cents), you make eight hundred naira ($4) per week, and one thousand six hundred naira ($8) in two weeks. So you make six hundred naira ($3) more than the store in your school by cutting your price by just two naira (1 cent). Is that not great?"

"That is great," Dangoma answered, smiling happily.

"Okay, it is getting late. Take your two packs of sweets and go do some business to make your uncle proud," Alhaji Kaswa said as he handed Dangoma two packs of Milky Nuts sweets.

"Thank you, Uncle Kaswa. I am really grateful. I now know why you are such a great businessman. When I grow up, I want to be like you and my uncle," Dangoma said as he handed Alhaji Kaswa the five hundred naira ($2.50 cents) for the two packs of sweets and ran home.

Chapter 9

Dangoma tries to sell sweets in school

Dangoma waited until break time before he told his friends he had sweets to sell. Initially, they were surprised.

"Dangoma, why do you want to sell sweets to us? We are your friends. You should share your sweets with us for free," Nanu, Dangoma's closest friend, said.

"Yes, Dangoma, we cannot buy sweets from you. You are our friend. You have to give them to us for free," said Maya, another of Dangoma's friends.

Dangoma struggled to explain to his friends why he had to sell the sweets.

"My uncle asked me to sell the sweets. I can't give them to you for free, but it is cheaper than what you can get in Malam's shop if you buy from me," Dangoma said.

But Dangoma's friends insisted that he give them the sweets for free.

Dangoma soon realised, to his surprise, that his friends would not buy the sweets from him no matter how well he explained why he had to sell the sweets. In fact, they were angry that their good friend was trying to sell them his sweets when he should have been sharing them for free.

Dangoma headed home sad that day. Not even one of his friends bought sweets from him; they all wanted them for free. His explanation that his uncle has asked him to sell the sweets did not appeal to his friends.

He was almost crying when he got home.

Dangoma's Mum consoles him

"Why are you looking so sad?" Dangoma's mummy asked when he got home.

"Nobody bought my sweets."

"Why?" she asked.

"They wanted them free because they are my friends," answered Dangoma.

"You should not be so sad. If you cannot sell sweets to your friends, let us look at a new set of people to whom you can sell the sweets."

"But who will buy them from me now?" Dangoma asked.

"Why not follow me to my shop today – that is, after you are through doing your homework. You can display your sweets besides my items in the shop. That way, you can market your sweets to my customers. Is that okay?"

"Okay," answered Dangoma.

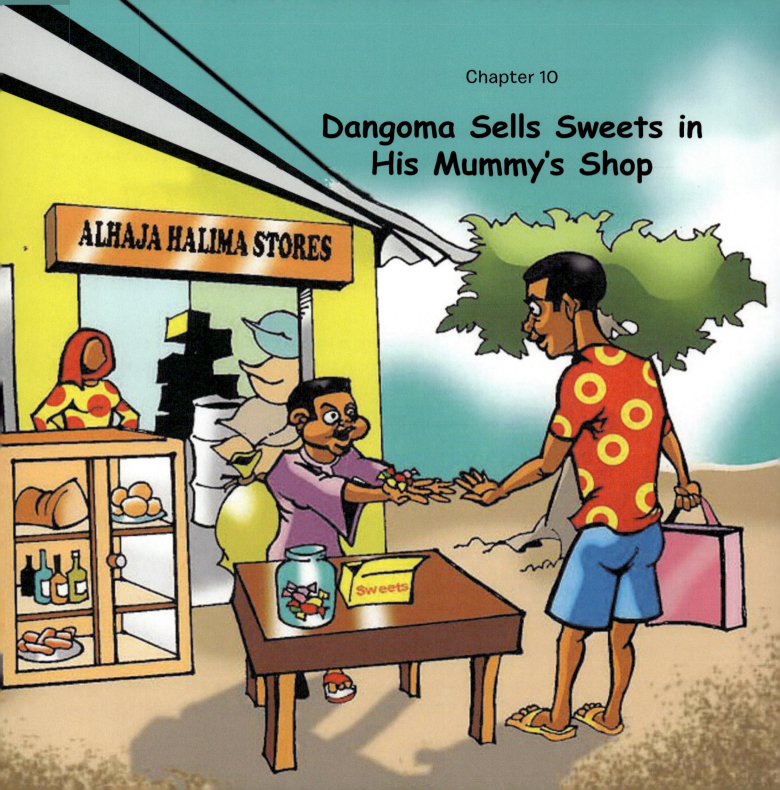

After lunch, Dangoma finished his homework quickly and followed his mummy to her shop.

Initially, it looked like no one was going to buy the sweets. Several customers came to the shop and bought things from Dangoma's mummy, but they said that they did not want to buy sweets.

Dangoma was beginning to feel sad again as the evening approached.

"Mummy, even your customers are not buying my sweets," Dangoma said sadly.

"Dangoma, be patient. Not all customers will want what you sell. Besides, today is just your first day here."

Later in the day, just as Dangoma was losing all hope that he was not going to sell his packs of sweets, a customer came into the shop, looked at Dangoma, and asked him what he was doing in the shop.

"I am selling sweets," Dangoma said.

"But your mummy does not sell sweets, so who gave you sweets to sell," the customer said.

"I am selling it for myself. I am learning to run a business," Dangoma answered.

"That is interesting. How much are you selling them for?" the customer asked.

"It is five hundred naira ($2.50) per pack," said Dangoma.

"That is too expensive. I am going to give you three hundred naira ($1.50) per pack. I will buy the two packs of sweets if you agree," the customer said.

Dangoma was confused, and he looked to his mummy for direction. His mummy was silent. He then looked at the customer and back at the sweets again. He knew he did not want to take the sweets home and tell Uncle Shangisha that he could not sell them.

Reluctantly, Dangoma said, "Okay."

Therefore, Dangoma sold the two packs for six hundred naira ($3), making a one hundred naira (50 cents) profit.

Immediately, he ran to tell Uncle Shangisha that he was only able to make one hundred naira (50 cents) profit on the five hundred naira ($2.50).

Uncle Shangisha took the money and shook his hand vigorously.

"Dangoma," Uncle Shangisha said, "you have done well. You have made your first profit in a business. I hope you are happy."

"I thought I could double the five hundred naira ($2.50)," Dangoma answered.

"Business is like that. Sometimes your expectation of profit will not be met immediately, but you must keep trying until you get the right customers that will buy from you at the right price."

He gave Dangoma back his one hundred naira (50 cents) profit, telling him that he would be a great businessman someday. He then asked Dangoma to sit down. Dangoma sat down expectantly, knowing his uncle always had something interesting to say about business.

"Listen, Dangoma, I can see you are sad about the fact that you did not make as much money as you expected in your first attempt at business. I am going to tell you the secrets of becoming successful. Hopefully, my words will guide and help you as you grow up," Uncle Shangisha said.

"First, if you want to succeed, you must not be afraid or ashamed to fail in business or in anything you do in life. Successful people look at failure as an opportunity to try again in a different way. They study why their initial attempt failed, and then they work out a better way to succeed."

"You need to understand why you could not sell sweets to your friends. Was it because they did not want to buy, or was it the way you tried to sell them?"

"I have not really thought about it," Dangoma answered.

"Start thinking about it," Uncle Shangisha said.

"Another secret to becoming successful is to think differently about a problem. Remember, every problem is also an opportunity that is waiting for you to exploit it. Always think of a solution when faced with a problem; never give up on a problem."

"The solutions do not have to be complex. Simple solutions to basic or complex issues in life can make you a lot of money."

Dangoma was nodding his head as the words of wisdom flowed from Uncle Shangisha.

"One reason you could not sell sweets to your friends is because you mixed business with emotions. Business and emotions do not go together usually. Business should be business, and if you offer value, you should be paid for it. If you decide to offer it for free, that is called charity."

"The other reason you sold your sweets so cheaply in your mother's shop is because you were desperate to sell. It's not surprising you could not get a very good price."

"I am going to give you the five hundred naira ($2.50) again. I want you to try to make as much profit as you can from it in the next week."

"Remember that, to be successful at anything you do, you must consistently work towards becoming successful. Success does not come as a gift; it comes to those who desire and work for it," Uncle Shangisha told Dangoma as he stood up to go.

Dangoma thanked his uncle and collected the five hundred naira ($2.50) again. He was feeling highly motivated with all that he had been told by his uncle. He was determined and confident that he could do better this time.

Chapter 12

Dangoma Tries Selling Sweets again

Motivated by the words of encouragement from his uncle, Dangoma headed straight to Alhaji Kaswa's shop to buy more sweets to sell.

Alhaji Kaswa was happy to see him.

"Welcome Dangoma. How are you doing? Alhaji Kaswa asked.

"Good afternoon! I am doing fine," Dangoma answered.

"How is business? I hope you were able to sell the sweets at a good profit."

"I was able to make one hundred naira (50 cents) profit on the two packs I bought from you," Dangoma answered.

"That is good, but I am sure you could have done better."

"Yes. Uncle Shangisha also says I could have done better," Dangoma said.

"Have you thought about what went wrong? Why you could not make as much money as you wished?"

"Uncle Shangisha said my friends were probably not the ideal people to try to sell sweets to because my emotions would affect my business decisions. He also said that I may have been too desperate to make a sale in my mummy's shop," Dangoma answered.

"That is true! Let me tell you something I did when I first started selling sweets. I knew there was nothing special about selling sweets. Every little shop I knew was selling them, but I still wanted to sell sweets because I loved them and knew many people who love them just as much. Therefore, to sell more sweets than every other person, I had to do something different that would make people buy sweets from me.

"So, I created a loyalty programme, which I still use today. If you buy ten sweets from me, you get the eleventh one free. The result is that I have a loyal group of customers who will not buy sweets anywhere else."

"But giving away free sweets means that I will make less profit," Dangoma protested.

"Yes, it means making less money now and more money later. Remember the concept of volume – because of the free sweet offer from me, I sell more sweets faster than my competitors. And because I sell more sweets, I make more profits than every other sweet seller in this market. That is why my shop is always full of people wanting to buy sweets."

"Wow! I have really learned a lot today from you and Uncle Shangisha."

"I really hope it helps you become a great business person eventually. You should always remember that success in business is not achieved overnight. Successful business people keep working and improving on their ideas until they become successful," Alhaji Kaswa said.

"Okay, I will remember that," answered Dangoma.

"Please do. Successful people are very optimistic people. Be positive. Always say to yourself, I can do it!" Be passionate and focus on achieving your goals. Do not complain about the obstacles in your way. If you cannot remove an obstacle in your way, look for a way to go around it."

"Thank you. I am really learning today," Dangoma responded.

"I am happy to hear you are learning. Now let us go back to the reason you are here. How many packs of sweets would you like to buy?" Alhaji Kaswa asked.

"I have six hundred naira. The five hundred naira Uncle Shangisha gave me and the one hundred naira profit I made. I would love to spend all of it buying sweets to sell." Dangoma answered.

"Okay. I am going to give you two packs of Milky Nuts sweets for the five hundred naira ($2.50), and I will give you a pack of Tintin sweets, which is one hundred naira (50 cents) a pack. Is that okay?" Alhaji Kaswa asked.

"Yes."

Chapter 13

Dangoma Makes a Second Attempt at Doing Business

Dangoma got home that day with the three packs of sweets bought from Alhaji Kaswa's shop.

He was confident that, with all the advice he had received from Uncle Shangisha and Alhaji Kaswa, he was better prepared to succeed in his second attempt at business.

He was particularly impressed with what Alhaji Kaswa told him about giving some sweets away for free to drive sales. Therefore, he decided that anyone who bought five milky nut sweets from him would get one tintin sweet for free. He also made up his mind not to sell the sweets in school because his friends wanted the sweets for free.

Ultimately, Dangoma begged his mum to allow him to have a small table outside her shop where he could display his sweets after school. Dangoma's mother agreed. And that is what he did once he had completed his homework one evening.

He also designed a big sign with the words Buy Five Sweets and Get One Free written on it in bold letters.

At first, sales were slow. As the day wore on, a few people bought some sweets and got a free Tintin sweet. And then more people started coming in to buy. Within an hour, Dangoma had finished selling both packs of sweets, making a profit of two hundred naira ($1).

He immediately ran to Alhaji Kaswa's shop to tell him the good news.

Alhaji Kaswa was so impressed that he offered Dangoma three packs of Milky Nuts sweets and a pack of Tintin sweets for just eight hundred and fifty naira ($4.27). Dangoma, however, had only eight hundred naira ($4).

"Dangoma, I am going to collect this eight hundred naira ($4) because you are becoming a regular customer. You are entitled to some credit facility from me now. Therefore, you can go away with the sweets. When you finish selling, pay me the balance of fifty naira (27 cents). All my regular customers enjoy the privilege of credit facility," Alhaji Kaswa said.

Dangoma was very happy, and he rushed home with the four packs of sweets.

The next day, he was at his mother's shop after school, and this time, the sweets sold out faster because many of those who bought from him the previous day came back to buy in addition to some new customers.

After five days of actively selling sweets in the evening, Dangoma had made two thousand naira ($10). He was happy, and he looked forward to meeting Uncle Shangisha on Sunday evening to tell him how much sales he had made from the five hundred naira ($2.50) he had been given to start his business.

Chapter 14

Dangoma Meets Uncle Shangisha again

It was a happy Dangoma who met Uncle Shangisha on Sunday evening.

"Uncle Shangisha," Dangoma called out as soon as he entered his house that evening, "I want tell you that I made one thousand four hundred naira ($7) profit from selling sweets this week."

"Dangoma, this is really great. I am really happy to hear that. What did you do differently this time that made you so successful?" Uncle Shangisha asked.

"I offered some free sweets to everyone who bought more than five sweets from me. I also designed a big sign that invited everyone to buy sweets from me. Plus, I went to mummy's friends' stores to sell sweets to them, and they all bought sweets from me."

"That is really good." Uncle Shangisha said. "You now see why it is good not to give up when you fail in business. You can always try again, but differently. I am really happy you are learning how to conduct business so quickly."

"Uncle, here is your five hundred naira ($2.50)," Dangoma said.

"Thank you," Uncle Shangisha said as he collected the money. Now what are you going to do with your one thousand five hundred naira ($7.50) profit?"

"I am going to buy more sweets to sell. I am also going to buy some biscuits because my mummy said those who buy sweets are likely to buy biscuits. I can easily sell both together," Dangoma answered.

"See, you are already expanding your business. That is really good. So you are going to be a sweet and biscuit merchant, and then, maybe later, you will add some fruit drinks, right?" Uncle Shangisha said.

"Yes. I really want to grow my business so that it will become as big as yours one day."

"I am really happy to hear that."

"You know, I am happy you are developing a vision. Every successful business starts with a vision. No business becomes successful by accident. It starts by setting a goal for yourself and working towards it. I am happy that you are already setting a goal for yourself," Uncle Shangisha told Dangoma.

"However, remember that setting a vision is not enough. You must show absolute dedication to that vision. This means using your time wisely. You cannot spend a good part of your time playing and expect to be successful."

He continued: "Successful people use their time wisely. If you want to be successful and rich in the future, Dangoma, you have to invest your time in things that will make you successful in the future. You must spend more of your time studying and on things that can make you even more money." For example, you can help your mummy in the shop when you are not studying," Uncle Shangisha said.

"Uncle, thank you. I am going to study and work hard," Dangoma answered.

"Dangoma, I have no doubt that you will work hard. However, working hard is usually not enough. Your hard work must breed success and earn you good money or else you are working hard in the wrong place. Remember this as you grow up: being rich is not a privilege, it is a right; however, it is a right you have to earn by creating value for society."

He continued: "Money has no bias in terms of your education, ethnicity, or social status. Money will come to you if you are able to create value for society. Don't just create value, learn to make money from the value you have created for society."

He then paused a moment before saying, "There are many ways you can create value in society. It can be as simple as selling sweets, or it can be as complex as trying to build a shuttle to satisfy people's desire to visit other planets in the universe. But whatever idea comes to you, pursue it with a passion and look for the best way to make money from it."

Finally, he added, "Many ordinary people think about money in terms of fear and scarcity. Those who become really rich are those who look at money through the eyes of freedom – the possibilities and opportunities that money can bring to you. My son, I want you to go out there and be successful. Do not look back."

Dangoma had sat quietly taking in all that Uncle Shangisha was telling him, and he left Uncle Shangisha's house thinking about what he had learned.

Chapter 15

Dangoma Opens a Bank Account

It was a happy Dangoma who ran to his mummy's shop after speaking with Uncle Shangisha. He met his mummy attending to a customer, but immediately after the customer had left, Dangoma said, "Mummy, Uncle Dangoma sends his greetings."

"That is good. I hope he is fine," replied Dangoma's mummy.

"Yes, he is fine. He has given me back the one thousand five hundred naira ($7.50) profit I made," Dangoma said, stretching his hands out to give the money to his mummy.

"That is really good. So what do you want to do with the money?"

"I want to do more business with it," answered Dangoma

"That is great, but let us take this a step forward. Let us go and open a bank account for you. There, you will save whatever money you make from your business."

"But do I really need a bank account, Mummy. I want you to be keeping my money for me," said Dangoma.

"Dangoma, you need a bank account, especially if you want to operate a larger business in the future. A bank is the best place to keep your money because your money will be safe and you will earn some interest on it," answered Dangoma's mummy.

"What is interest?"

"Interest is the money the bank pays you for keeping your money with them. It is usually a percentage of whatever money you have with them. For example, for your one thousand five hundred naira ($7.50), the bank may decide to pay you 5 per cent interest every year," answered Dangoma's mummy.

"But why would the bank pay me interest for keeping my money?" asked Dangoma.

"Banks pay you interest because they lend your deposited money to those who need money for business and other purposes, and they charge the borrowers interest. The interest they charge borrowers is usually higher than what they pay depositors, so the bank makes profit from the difference between the lower interest rate they pay depositors and the higher interest rate they charge borrowers."

"Does that mean I can also borrow money from the bank for my business?" Dangoma asked.

"Yes, Dangoma. By opening a bank account now, you will be able to build a strong relationship with the bank. That way, when you need money to expand your business someday, you can borrow money from them," answered Dangoma's mummy.

"This is really interesting," Dangoma replied.

"Dangoma, let us go so that I can open the bank account for you. I am taking you to my bank. I have been banking with them for many years now. They are good because they also support my business. I am sure they will support your business someday too." She then locked up her shop, grabbed Dangoma's hand, and walked to the bank just across the road from her shop.

At the bank, Dangoma was impressed with the smartly dressed bankers who attended to him. His mum filled out all the forms on his behalf, and within a few minutes, he was told that an account had been opened in his name.

"Dangoma, I am going to put half of your one thousand five hundred naira ($7.50) in your new bank account. You can use the remaining seven hundred and fifty naira ($3.25) to continue your business. As you make more money, you can save more money in your bank account."

Chapter 16

Dangoma Studies Business and Becomes a Billionaire

After thirsting for business success, Dangoma made a decision to learn more about business. With his seven hundred and fifty naira ($3.25), he set up a small table in his mother's shop where he sold sweets and then biscuits and then fruit drinks.

His small business grew. Soon, he took over his mother's shop selling sweets, biscuits, and fruit drinks. Quickly, he was making enough money to pay part of his school fees.

But Dangoma never neglected his schoolwork despite doing well in business. He studied hard and passed his examinations at the university where he studied business administration.

In his studies, he was taught the science of managing a business and how to sell products. He studied hard and completed his degree with flying colours.

After university, Uncle Shangisha loaned him some money to start a business. He set up a small business where he started selling sugar because he believed everyone loved sugar.

Soon, applying many of things he learned in school and from Uncle Shangisha and Alhaji Kaswa, his business grew and grew. Eventually, Dangoma became the biggest sugar merchant in town.

With his sugar business now big, Dangoma opened other businesses, which also became highly successful.

Whenever he was asked about the secret of his success, he told people about Alhaji Kaswa, his mummy, and Uncle Shangisha: "Alhaji Kaswa taught me pricing, volume strategy, and how to make more profits than the competition. My mummy taught me marketing and the will to persevere. Uncle Shangisha was my inspiration and mentor."

Activity Sheet

1. **Imagine you have been asked to start a small business in your school. Pick a friend with whom you would like to go into that business with, sit down with him or her, and discuss what that business will be and how you will orchestrate matters. Consider the following questions:**

   a. Which products or services are you going to sell or offer?

   b. How much will you need to start the business?

   c. To whom will you sell your products or services?

   d. How are you going to market these products or services?

   e. How will you arrive at the final sales price of your products or services?

   f. What would a cash flow statement (which shows how much money you will make on a monthly basis within the next six months if your products or services are successful) look like for your business?

About the Book

Dangoma grew up daydreaming about becoming a billionaire like his rich relative, Uncle Shangisha. He gets a break when Uncle Shangisha gives him N500 ($2.50) to start a business when he is just ten years old. Dangoma soon finds out that running a business is not as easy as he imagined, but he learns several business concepts like pricing, marketing, and patience. Along the way, he discovers the secrets necessary to become a very successful business person. This book is aimed at teaching basic business concepts to both primary and secondary school students in an accessible way. The aim is to stir in students an interest in business and fuel their entrepreneurial zeal while they are still young.

About the Author

Anthony Osae-Brown is a financial journalist and communication professional with over fourteen years of experience writing about economic and financial issues in Nigeria and working in the communication departments of leading banks. He has a deep understanding of global economic and financial issues, especially as they relate to Nigerian and West African economies.

He has worked with leading newspapers such as BusinessDay, Nigeria's leading business newspaper, and Mergermarket (formerly, the financial intelligence news service of The Financial Times). He contributes regularly to the BBC on matters concerning the economy and is consulted frequently by foreign firms conducting due diligence on Nigerian companies or individuals seeking a perspective on economic issues related to Nigeria and West Africa.

As a communication professional who has worked with leading financial institutions, he has used his strong writing skills to shape the brand perception and reputation of some of Nigeria's leading banks, which has resulted in significant improvement in product sales. He knows a great deal about financial communication and economic analysis.

Anthony holds a first degree in finance from the University of Ilorin, Nigeria, and a master's degree in financial journalism from the University of Stirling, Scotland. He is married and has two beautiful children.

Printed in the United States
By Bookmasters